100 FACTS YOU SHOULD KNOW

ARCHAEOLOGY

John Farndon
Consultant: Ethan Cochrane

Gareth Stevens
PUBLISHING

Please visit our website, www.garethstevens.com. For a free color catalog of all our high-quality books, call toll free 1-800-542-2595 or fax 1-877-542-2596.

Cataloging-in-Publication Data

Names: Farndon, John. | Cochrane, Ethan, consultant.
Title: Archaeology / John Farndon; consultant, Ethan Cochrane.
Description: New York : Gareth Stevens Publishing, 2016. | Series: 100 facts you should know | Includes index.
Identifiers: ISBN 9781482451382 (pbk.) | ISBN 9781482451320 (library bound) | ISBN 9781482451207 (6 pack)
Subjects: LCSH: Archaeology--Miscellanea--Juvenile literature.
Classification: LCC CC171.F37 2016 | DDC 930.1--dc23

Published in 2017 by
Gareth Stevens Publishing
111 East 14th Street, Suite 349
New York, NY 10003

Copyright © 2017 Miles Kelly Publishing Ltd.

Publishing Director: Belinda Gallagher
Creative Director: Jo Cowan
Assistant Editor: Carly Blake
Volume Designer: Andrea Slane
Cover Designer: Simon Lee
Image Manager: Lorraine King
Indexer: Jane Parker
Production: Elizabeth Collins, Caroline Kelly
Reprographics: Stephan Davis, Jennifer Cozens, Thom Allaway
Assets: Lorraine King

Acknowledgements:

The publishers would like to thank the following artists who have contributed to this book: Mike Foster, Andrea Morandi, Mike Saunders.

All other artwork from the Miles Kelly Artwork Bank

The publishers would like to thank the following sources for the use of their photographs:
Cover Javier Etcheverry/VW PICS; Page 6 Jonathan Blair/Corbis; 9(br)(tr) Louise Murray/Science Photo Library; 11 Deloche Lissac/Godong/Corbis; 12(tl) Mary Evans Picture Library/Alamy; 13 Kevin Schafer/Corbis; 14(t) John Reader/Science Photo Library, (b) Phil Yeomans/Rex Features; 15 Silkeborg Museum, Denmark/Munoz-Yague/Science Photo Library; 17(t) Sipa Press/Rex Features; 20 Yann Arthus-Bertrand/Corbis; 21(t) Andreas Manolis/Reuters/Corbis, (b) AFP/Getty Images; 24(t) Richard T. Nowitz/Corbis, (cr) vphoto/Fotolia.com, (b) Peter Brooker/Rex Features; 26(t) David Gallimore/Alamy, (b) John Reader/Science Photo Library; 27(tr)(b) Sipa Press/Rex Features; 29(tl) Hulton-Deutsch Collection/Corbis; 30(br) Jean Dominique Dallet/Alamy, (tr) Dragon News/Rex Features; 31(tl) Dragon News/Rex Features; 32 inopix/Rex Features; 33 Werner Forman/Corbis; 34 Alexis Rosenfeld/Science Photo Library; 35 Jens Benninghofen/Alamy; 36 Courtesy of APVA Preservation Virginia; 37(tr) York Archaeological Trust, (b) Charles O'Rear/Corbis; 40(t) Adam Woolfitt/Robert Harding/Rex Features, (b) ©webbaviation.co.uk; 41(c) Danita Delimont/Alamy, (b) Jgz/Fotolia.com; 45 National Geographic/Getty Images; 46 map Gary Hincks/Science Photo Library, (b) Emmanuel Laurent/Eurelios/Science Photo Library; 47 Homer Sykes Archive/Alamy

All other photographs are from: Corel, digitalSTOCK, digitalvision, iStockphoto.com, John Foxx, PhotoAlto, PhotoDisc, PhotoEssentials, PhotoPro, Stockbyte

Printed in the United States of America

CPSIA compliance information: Batch CS16GS: For further information contact Gareth Stevens, New York, New York at 1-800-542-2595.

Contents

The past beneath us

1 **An archaeologist's job is to find out about people in ancient times.** They look for ancient things buried in the ground. Whether they find amazing objects or just old trash, each piece gives vital clues to what life was like.

▼ Archaeologists work on a dig at Calico Hills, California. They carefully scrape away the earth, recording every thing they find that might help them build up a picture of the past.

Digging into the past

2 **Archaeologists uncover the past by digging.** In many places the ground is filled with debris that has piled up over time, so they have to dig down to reach the oldest layers. As they dig, archaeologists study each piece of debris they find – the smallest item may tell them something.

▼ Archaeologists use special tools, such as brushes and small trowels, so as not to damage vital evidence during a dig.

METAL DETECTING

You can hunt for buried treasure with a metal detector*. You must have permission to use it though, so why not start in your back garden? You may find an old spoon or tin, but you may just come across something special!
Always get an adult to help you.

*Metal detectors suitable for children to use can be bought cheaply.

3 **A "dig" is marked out with a grid.** Archaeologists tie lengths of string across the dig site, making a pattern of squares. This means they can record the square in which they made their find. The position an object is found in provides extra clues.

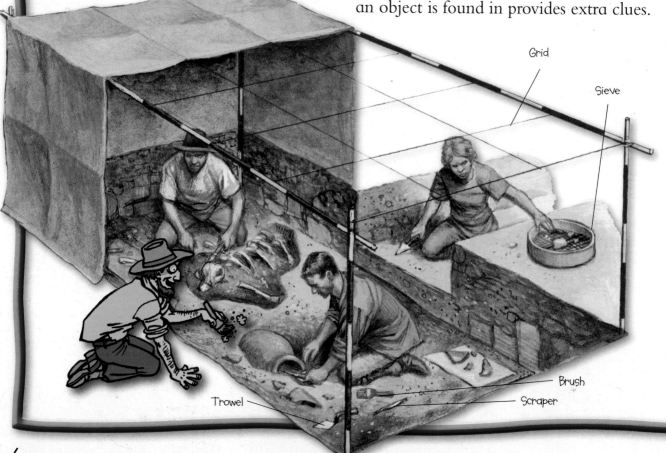

Grid

Sieve

Brush

Scraper

Trowel

4 **Archaeologists use science to see into the ground.** By sending radar waves into the earth with a special machine, archaeologists can detect things hidden below the surface. This is called geophysics. The picture it builds up indicates the best places to start digging.

▲ The fuzz on the "geophys" machine screen reveals the shadow of ancient structures underground.

▶ An archaeologist runs a "geophys" check using ground-penetrating radar to see where to start digging.

5 **Metal detectors reveal buried metal objects.** They send an electrical and magnetic signal into the earth and when metal is found, they click loudly. Amateur archaeologists enjoy hunting for coins and other treasures with a metal detector.

▲ Metal detectors can detect metal objects beneath the ground.

Reconstruction

▼▶ The crumpled 3,500-year-old Ringlemere Cup was found using a metal detector. A reconstruction was made to show what it would have looked like.

As it was found

How old is it?

6 The deeper an object is buried, the older it is likely to be. Garbage and other objects thrown away build up in layers over many years. The layer an object is found in can show how old it is.

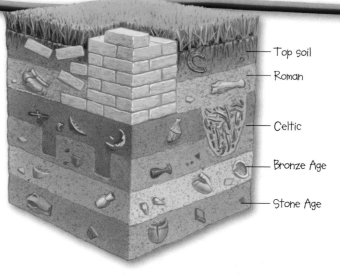

- Top soil
- Roman
- Celtic
- Bronze Age
- Stone Age

▲ Going down through the layers in the ground is like going further into the past.

COUNTING TREE RINGS

You will need:

• ruler • notebook • pen

Find a cut tree trunk. Measure the width of each ring and write it down. Multiply each measurement by ten, and using a ruler, draw the measurements as a bar chart. Do the same for other tree trunks you find. Compare your charts to see if you find a matching pattern. If they match, you have found matching years.

7 The rings of a tree show its yearly growth. Scientists have worked out a chart for the pattern of tree rings over the last 7,500 years. When archaeologists find a piece of old wood, they look for a matching pattern of rings on the chart to tell its age.

▼ The number of rings in a tree trunk show how old the tree is.

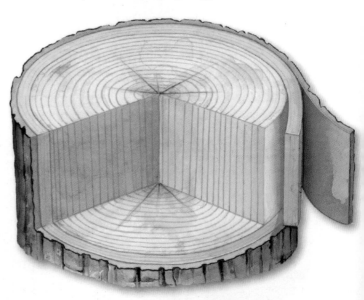

8 Scientists find out how old pottery is by heating it. Pottery soaks up particles called electrons from its surroundings. Scientists take a fragment of pottery and heat it up. The older it is and the more electrons it contains, the brighter it glows. This is called thermoluminescence.

▼ When animals die, the carbon 14 in their bodies starts to leak away.

Animals take in carbon 14 when they eat plants

After death, carbon 14 begins to leak away steadily

The amount of carbon 14 in remains can give an accurate time of death

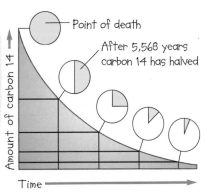
Point of death

After 5,568 years carbon 14 has halved

Amount of carbon 14

Time

9 Dead plants and animals have built-in clocks.

All living things contain something called carbon 14. When they die, it leaks away at a steady rate, like a ticking clock. The amount of carbon 14 left in the remains tells scientists how long ago something died. This is called carbon dating.

▲ This curve shows the decay of carbon 14 in animal and plant remains. The amount of carbon 14 never reaches zero.

10 Experts must be careful with carbon dating.

Legend says a cloth called the Turin Shroud covered Jesus Christ after he died. In 1988, scientists dated the shroud to AD 1300 – 1,300 years after Christ's death. It seemed to be a fake. Others say the scientists tested a repair patch, added in AD 1300 – could the rest of the cloth be much older?

▶ Some scientists say carbon dating proves the Turin Shroud is a medieval fake. Others still believe it is genuine.

Buried treasure

11 **Heinrich Schliemann's discovery brought the city of Troy to life.** An ancient Greek story tells how Troy was destroyed by fire about 1200 BC. In 1870, Schliemann found the charred remains of buildings when he dug near Hissarlik, Turkey. He also found treasure he believed had belonged to the famous King Priam of Troy.

◀ Schliemann's wife Sophia wearing some of the jewels, known as "the Jewels of Helen."

12 **The Snettisham Treasure was buried by British kings over 2,000 years ago.** Dozens of gold and silver torcs (neck rings) were found at Snettisham in England in 1948. They probably belonged to kings of the Iceni people who lived in southern Britain and may have been buried for safekeeping.

13 **In 1987, archaeologists discovered a tomb in Peru filled with fantastic gold treasures.** The tomb was found at Sipán in Peru. It belonged to a lord of the Moche people who lived in Peru between 100 BC and AD 700. Other Moche tombs found previously had been robbed of their treasures. The Sipán tomb was the first to be found intact with all its treasures.

14 The Ardagh Chalice was found in Ireland in 1868 by two boys digging for potatoes. Dating back to the 8th century, it is made of silver and decorated with gold and brass. It was just buried in the soil, so the original owner may have hidden it hurriedly for safekeeping – but never came back to find it!

▼ Unearthed at Sipán in Mexico was the most fabulous ancient treasure ever found in the Americas.

▲ The beautiful Ardagh Chalice is the finest example of 8th century metalwork ever to have been discovered.

Human remains

15 Archaeologists can tell a great deal about ancient people from just a few bone fragments. A wider pelvis is likely to have been a woman's and the length of a thigh bone shows a person's height. With young people, teeth can reveal their age. Microscopic and chemical tests on bones can also show what diseases people suffered from.

16 Bones can last for millions of years when fossilized. In 1974, scientists found fossilized bones in Ethiopia. The bones were 3.2 million years old and belonged to a small female creature. The scientists called her Lucy. She was a bit like a human and a bit like an ape, and just 3.3 feet (1 m) tall. Lucy was one of our first ancestors.

▲ The discovery of Lucy's bones was a vital clue to human ancestry.

▼ Teeth reveal how old someone was when they died, because different teeth appear as people grow older.

MAKING FOOTPRINTS

At Laetoli in Ethiopia, scientists found 3.75 million-year-old footprints preserved in volcanic ash. The distance between each step showed they were made by a creature the same size as Lucy. When you walk on a beach, measure the distance between your footprints. Compare it with an adult's footprints.

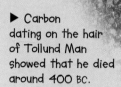

▶ Carbon dating on the hair of Tollund Man showed that he died around 400 BC.

17 **Peat bogs can preserve bodies for thousands of years.** In 1950, two villagers from Tollund in Denmark found a man's body while digging peat. Police thought he was a recent murder victim. However scientists worked out the man was murdered 2,500 years ago! Over 1,000 prehistoric "bog bodies" have been found.

18 **In 1991, two walkers found a frozen body in the Alpine Mountains in Northern Italy.** They thought the body was an unlucky climber. In fact, the body was 5,300 years old. The mountain ice had preserved the body like food in a freezer. Scientists nicknamed the body Ötzi the Iceman. Ötzi has taught us a lot about life 5,300 years ago.

◀ Ötzi the Iceman is the oldest mummified human body to be found in Europe.

19 **When archaeologists find a skull, they may want to know what a person looked like.** Scientists can recreate a face by building up layers of muscle and features in modeling clay or on a computer. The recreated face is then revealed as it may have looked when the person was alive.

Reading clues

20 **Pollen grains provide clues to the past.** Plants rot quickly after they die, but their pollen grains can last for thousands of years. By identifying ancient pollen, scientists can tell what plants were growing and what foods people ate.

▲ Pollen grains can show how a land was settled long ago as farmers planted different crops.

21 **Ancient writing can be very revealing — if you can read it.** No one could read Egyptian hieroglyphs until the Rosetta Stone was found 200 years ago. A passage of text is carved on it in three ancient languages, including hieroglyphs. By comparing the texts, scholars painstakingly worked out what each hieroglyph meant.

▶ The Rosetta Stone is an official order of the ancient Egyptian King Ptolemy V. The order is written in hieroglyphics, demotic Egyptian (simpler than hieroglyphics) and ancient Greek. The stone has enabled us to understand hieroglyphic writing.

▲ Reconstructing ancient pots from tiny pieces is like doing a jigsaw puzzle in three dimensions – with the pieces from different puzzles mixed up!

22 **Pottery breaks, but the pieces last forever.** Archaeologists often find bits of broken pottery. It may look like garbage, but an expert can tell who made it and when – just from a tiny piece. Many peoples in the past are known mainly by the pottery they left.

23 **Roman pottery jars called amphorae were used like tin cans are today.** Amphorae were used for carrying wine, olive oil, fish sauce, nuts, meat, lime and pitch. Archaeologists find bits of amphorae all around the Mediterranean. Powerful microscopes and chemical tests reveal what they held from thin traces left on the clay.

▶ Amphorae tell archaeologists a great deal about what the Romans ate and drank.

15

Mounds and monuments

24 **Many people built large mounds to bury their dead leaders.** One of the most famous burial mounds is Newgrange in Ireland. It was built about 5,000 years ago, and inside there is a passage that leads to a stone burial chamber. Archaeologists have partly uncovered it.

▲ The entrance to the passage to Newgrange in Ireland has an ancient decorated stone in front of it.

25 **Ancient burial mounds in England are called barrows.** Those built 5,000–6,000 years ago are long and narrow. Barrows were used to bury important families. Those built about 4,000 years ago are round and were built to bury a single chieftain or king.

Central passage

Burial chambers

Huge stones seal the entrance

◀ The West Kennet long barrow in Wiltshire was in use from 3600–2500 BC and at least 46 people were buried there.

26
An ancient mound in Ohio is shaped like a snake. Many native peoples in ancient Ohio built mounds, including the snake-shaped Great Serpent Mound. A few were used for burials but no one knows what most of them were for.

▲ This may be how ancient people erected the huge stones of Stonehenge, but scientists don't know for sure.

27
Over 3,500 years ago in Europe, huge standing stones called megaliths were put up in circles. Stonehenge in Wiltshire is the most famous stone circle. Some experts think they were places for ceremonies or temples. Others say they were huge calendars for tracking the Sun through the year.

28
The world's oldest stone circle is in the desert. Most stone circles are in western Europe, but the oldest is in the Nubian desert of Egypt, in a region called Nabta Playa. This stone circle is 1,000 years older than Stonehenge. Experts say it was a temple where cattle were sacrificed.

QUIZ
1. How old is Ireland's Newgrange?
2. Who was buried in a round barrow?
3. What is a megalith?

Answers:
1. 5,000 years old
2. A chieftain or king 3. A large standing stone

17

The oldest things

29 Under a mound at Çatal Hüyük in Turkey, 8,000-year-old remains of a town were found. The houses were close together and there were no streets, so people got into their homes by a hole in the roof!

▲ This mound near Çatal Hüyük in Turkey contains the remains of the world's oldest town.

▼ Çatal Hüyük had no streets. People walked across the rooftops to get to their houses.

30 The oldest religion worshipped pythons. In 2006, archaeologist Sheila Coulson found a cave in the Tsodilo Hills of Botswana, Africa. Inside was a stone carved in the shape of a python. Stone tools nearby showed it was carved over 70,000 years ago. This means the cave is the world's oldest religious site.

MAKING DATES

Draw a chart with dates along the bottom. Find the three oldest things in your room and plot their age on the chart. Repeat with the three oldest things in your house, in your neighborhood and in your city or region. Use books, the Internet and museums to help you find dates.

31 **The ancient Greeks must have smelled awful!** In 2007, archaeologists found an ancient perfume factory at Pyrgos in Cyprus. Over 4,000 years ago, people were making scores of huge jars of perfume. From traces in the jars, scientists recreated the perfume – it was very strong.

32 **Remains of the world's oldest boat were found in the desert.** Tar-coated bundles of reeds covered in barnacles were found at As-Sabiyah in Kuwait, in the Arabian desert. They are 7,000 years old. At that time there were rivers in the desert, but they have since dried up.

▲ These bits of broken pottery come from jars that were used to make perfume 4,000 years ago.

33 **In June 2008, archaeologists found what is perhaps the world's oldest Christian church.** It was in a hidden cave under a newer church in Rihab, Jordan. Those who discovered it say the cave was used as a church 2,000 years ago – when Christ was said to have lived.

▶ Archaeologists who discovered this hidden cave believe it was used as a church by Christ's disciples nearly 2,000 years ago.

Ancient weapons

34 **Two million years ago, people sharpened stones by chipping the edges.** These stones were used as tools such as axes and spears. This time in history is called the Stone Age. It lasted up until about 3300 BC when metals were discovered.

▶ Stone Age people hunted with stone-tipped wooden spears and stone axes.

35 **Half a million years ago, Europeans hunted large animals with spears.** At that time there were rhinoceroses and elephant-like animals in Europe. A 500,000-year-old rhino shoulder bone was found at Boxgrove in England. It had a spear wound. People living at that time were brave to hunt such large animals with just wooden spears.

▼ Archaeologists divide prehistoric times into three ages by the materials people used to make tools. These dates apply to the Near East (where bronze and iron were first discovered), but the three ages can be identified elsewhere in the world.

STONE AGE approximately up until 3300 BC
Humans mainly used stone to make tools and weapons, although wood and bone were also used.

BRONZE AGE approximately 3300–1200 BC
Metal started to be widely used. Bronze was smelted from tin and copper ores. It is hard wearing and ideal for weapons and armor.

IRON AGE approximately 1200–500 BC
As better smelting techniques developed, iron started to be widely used. Iron was widely available.

QUIZ

1. What were the first weapons made of?
2. What metals are mixed to make bronze?
3. What was more available: iron or bronze?

Answers:
1. Stone
2. Copper and tin 3. Iron

36
People began using metal about 5,300 years ago. Some rocks contain metal. When they are heated, the metal melts and it can be molded into items such as pots or swords. Copper is a soft metal, but adding tin makes bronze, which is much tougher. With this discovery a new period of history began – the Bronze Age.

◀ A bronze worker is pouring molten (liquid) metal into a clay mold to set.

▶ By 1000 BC, metal swords and other weapons were being made all over Europe and western Asia.

37
Ancient Celts flung swords into water. The story of King Arthur tells how he hurled his sword Excalibur into a lake. It might be based on truth. At Flag Fen in Cambridgeshire, England, some 3,000-year-old swords were found in a pool. People donated the swords to water, just as people today throw coins in fountains.

38
About 3,500 years ago, ancient people called Hittites discovered iron. This metal is only a little tougher than bronze, which was costly. Iron meant armies of peasants could be armed with cheap swords. A new period of history called the Iron Age had begun.

Bronze sword

Iron sword

◀ As more and more countries were able to arm their armies during the Iron Age, wars happened much more frequently.

Food from the past

39 **Sometimes, whole meals are preserved from ancient times.** When Mount Vesuvius erupted in 79 BC, it covered the Roman city of Pompeii in ash. It happened so quickly that uneaten meals were preserved under the ash. Priests in the Temple of Isis were eating grilled fish and eggs at the time.

▲ This bowl of olives was found preserved in the ruins of Pompeii.

40 **Burned food may taste horrible but it lasts!** Food rots quickly, but if it was burned it can last for thousands of years. By studying ancient, charred food under microscopes scientists can tell if it came from farmed or wild plants. This was how it was discovered that rice was first farmed in China 11,500 years ago on the Yangtze River.

41 **Lindow Man showed what Iron Age people cooked.** He is one of several ancient bodies that have been found preserved in peat bogs. Scientists studied the contents of his stomach – he had eaten a bran cake cooked for half an hour at 200°C on a hot, flat pan!

▲ Flat bread, similar to the bran cake Lindow Man ate, is the oldest of all prepared foods.

▼ The body of Lindow Man was found in Cheshire, England. Tests show he died in the first century AD.

▶ Sunflowers were perhaps the first crop grown by Native Americans in North America.

Sunflower seeds

Hazelnuts

42 The world's oldest cooking fire was found in a cave in South Africa.

Swartkrans is a cave in South Africa's Transvaal region. Inside the cave, scientists found animal bones that had been burned in a camp fire 1.5 million years ago. The cooked bones belonged to antelopes, zebras and warthogs.

▼▶ Before farming, people gathered foods such as fruits and nuts and hunted wild animals.

Apples

43 Scanning ancient plates for chemical traces reveals what people ate.

In the 2,700-year-old tomb of King Midas in Turkey, archaeologists found cups and plates. Tests on them revealed minute traces of food. They showed that at Midas' funeral they ate barbecued lamb and lentils, and drank wine sweetened with honey and spiced with fennel and anise.

▼▶ People began to hunt animals for food. Small animals such as rabbits and boar could be hunted by one man. To kill larger animals, men would hunt in a group.

Rabbit

Wild boar

44 Old bones tell archaeologists what people's favorite foods were.

Bones may look old and dry, but they can reveal a lot about a person. By analyzing certain atoms, scientists can tell what a person ate. Bones found in Venezuela showed when people there stopped eating roots and started growing and eating corn (about 2,000 years ago).

▶ People found a more reliable food supply as they learned to plant and grow seeds such as peas and chickpeas. They also planted wild grasses, which became wheat and barley.

Peas

Chickpeas

Faking it

45 **Ancient South American crystal skulls are probably fakes.** Many museums display these skulls, which are said to have been made by the ancient peoples of America. Some say they have mysterious powers but they were probably made by modern stonecutters.

46 **Piltdown Man was a famous hoax.** In 1912, an archaeologist found bits of a skull in Piltdown quarry in Sussex, England. The skull was said to be one million years old and proved the link between humans and apes. Forty years later, scientists showed it was just an old human skull with an orangutan's jawbone!

▲ Tests showed many "ancient Aztec" crystal skulls such as this were fake.

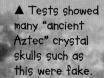

▲ "Ancient" human bones dug up in Piltdown quarry were planted there by a hoaxer.

◄ The lower right canine tooth of Piltdown man.

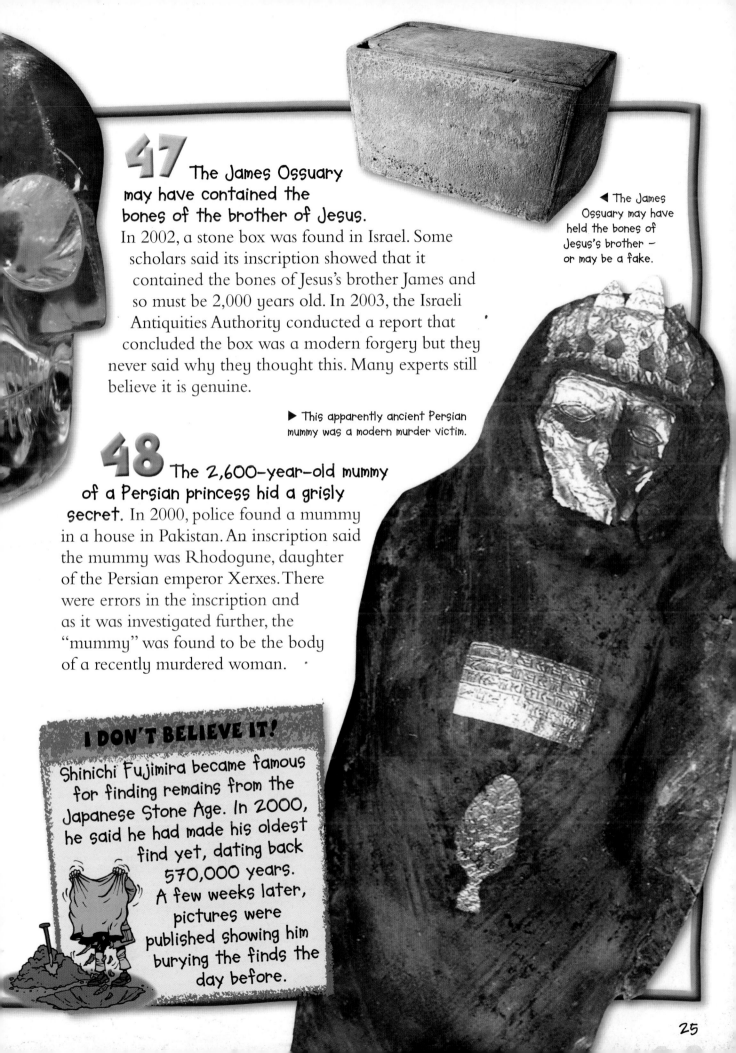

47 The James Ossuary may have contained the bones of the brother of Jesus.

In 2002, a stone box was found in Israel. Some scholars said its inscription showed that it contained the bones of Jesus's brother James and so must be 2,000 years old. In 2003, the Israeli Antiquities Authority conducted a report that concluded the box was a modern forgery but they never said why they thought this. Many experts still believe it is genuine.

◄ The James Ossuary may have held the bones of Jesus's brother – or may be a fake.

► This apparently ancient Persian mummy was a modern murder victim.

48 The 2,600-year-old mummy of a Persian princess hid a grisly secret.

In 2000, police found a mummy in a house in Pakistan. An inscription said the mummy was Rhodogune, daughter of the Persian emperor Xerxes. There were errors in the inscription and as it was investigated further, the "mummy" was found to be the body of a recently murdered woman.

I DON'T BELIEVE IT!

Shinichi Fujimira became famous for finding remains from the Japanese Stone Age. In 2000, he said he had made his oldest find yet, dating back 570,000 years. A few weeks later, pictures were published showing him burying the finds the day before.

Hunting for pharaohs

49 **The Great Pyramid of Giza in Egypt is the world's biggest building.** It was built 4,500 years ago as a tomb for the pharaoh Khufu. Yet even with modern technology, experts cannot find Khufu's resting place inside.

▲ The huge stone pyramids at Giza were built as tombs for Egyptian pharaohs.

50 **The only pharaoh's tomb ever found intact was Tutankhamun's, who lived 3,300 years ago.** Egyptians buried kings with treasures to help them through the afterlife. Many tombs were robbed, but in 1922 archaeologists found the tomb of the boy-king intact. Inside were the most amazing treasures ever found.

◄ This fabulous gold mask was made to cover the face of Tutankhamun's mummy.

51 When archaeologist Howard Carter opened Tutankhamun's tomb, it was said he unleashed a curse. Carter's pet canary was killed by a cobra the day the tomb was opened. The dig's patron, Lord Carnarvon — and his dog — also died soon after. It was said to be the "Mummy's Curse." However, Carter lived long after.

◀ Howard Carter opening Tutankhamun's tomb in 1922.

52 The Egyptian queen, Nefertiti, was said to be extremely beautiful. Nefertiti was the wife of Akhenaten, Tutankhamun's father. They founded a city in the desert but only a bust of her has survived, showing how beautiful she was.

53 The body of the Egyptian king Ramses II is over 4,000 years old. The ancient Egyptians used special fluids to preserve the bodies of important people when they died. In 1817, archaeologist Giovanni Battista Belzoni found the mummy of the greatest Egyptian king, Ramses II.

▶ Nefertiti was the stepmother of Tutankhamun. Her name means "the beautiful one has come."

High-tech history

54 The ancient Greeks made a computer 2,200 years ago. In 1901, in a shipwreck off the Greek island of Antikythera, a box containing bronze gears and dials was found. Scientists figured out that these parts made up a mechanical computer, used to work out the position of the Moon and stars.

Iron rod

Copper cylinder

◀ The reconstructed Baghdad Battery produced a current when grape juice was added.

▲ The crusted lumps of the Antikythera find don't look that interesting, but an X-ray revealed the complex gears of this ancient computer (above).

55 The oldest battery was made 2,000 years before the electric flashlight was invented! In the 1930s, a clay pot was found in Baghdad, Iraq. Inside was a copper cylinder and an iron rod – similar to a modern flashlight battery. Batteries need acid to work, so when scientists recreated the pot, they poured in acidic grape juice. Amazingly, the pot produced an electric current!

Acidic liquid such as grape juice or vinegar

56 Did the ancient Egyptians have electric lights? In Dendera Temple near Luxor, Egypt, strange pictures are carved on the wall. They show long tubes with squiggles inside. Some experts say they could be light bulbs but few agree.

▶ A carving in Dendera Temple, Egypt. Some experts think the long tube in the carving is an ancient light bulb.

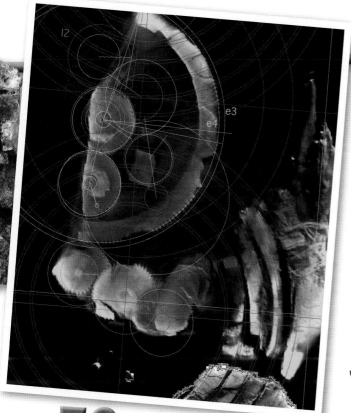

57

The earliest jet engine was invented 2,000 years before the first plane took off. Drawings made by the Greek thinker Hero 2,100 years ago show a flask of water with spouts on the side. When it is heated from below, steam jets out from the spouts and makes the flask spin around. Modern jet engines work in the same way, except that the jet is made by burning fuel.

▼ Hero's aeolipile. Jets of steam shooting from the pipes would have made the globe whiz round.

58

The ancient Egyptians made a model plane. In 1898, archaeologists found a toy in a tomb at Saqqara, Egypt. At the time, it was put away in a box and left for almost a century. When Dr. Khalil Messiha looked at the model in 1969 he was astonished to find it looked similar to a modern plane, yet it was 2,200 years old!

QUIZ

1. What did scientists pour into the reconstructed Baghdad Battery?
2. Where was the Antikythera Mechanism found?
3. What did the bird model found at Saqqara look like?

Answers:
1. Acidic grape juice 2. In a shipwreck off the Greek island of Antikythera 3. A modern plane

Ancient China

59 **China is the most ancient surviving civilization.** Its history dates back over 4,000 years. Other civilizations, such as ancient Egypt, started earlier, but crumbled long ago. Only China has survived into modern times.

60 **China's oldest people were lost in the war.** In the 1920s, archaeologists found dozens of 400,000-year-old skulls of China's oldest inhabitants at Zhoukoudian, near Beijing. They called them Peking or Beijing Man. The skulls strangely vanished during World War II. No one has seen them since.

I DON'T BELIEVE IT!

Mount Li, Emperor Huangdi's burial mound, has yet to be opened but may contain a vast model city. Legends say it contains rivers of flowing mercury, and lethal booby traps, such as armed crossbows, to protect the emperor's last resting place.

◄ The 3,000-year-old "dragon bones" are the earliest records of Chinese writing.

61 **The oldest relics of Chinese writing are the "dragon bones" of Yinxu.** A century ago, ancient bones with symbols on them were found at Yinxu in China. Locals said they were dragon bones, but they were actually the bones of deer and oxen. The bones date back over 3,000 years and are now known as "oracle bones" because they provided people with oracles (advice from the gods).

62 **The first Chinese emperor was buried with a life-sized army.** When he died, Qin Shi Huangdi (259–210 BC) was buried in a vast tomb complex. In 1974, archaeologists uncovered the broken remains of an army of 7,500 full-sized warriors, horses and chariots made from terracotta clay. The emperor's tomb has not yet been explored, but it may contain more marvels.

◄ The soldiers in the terracotta army were once painted in bright colors. Each one is slightly different and may be based on a real person.

▲ The Chinese used gunpowder for firing weapons.

63 **The Chinese were great inventors.** They invented the magnetic compass 1,000 years before it appeared in Europe. They also invented paper and printing. About 1,200 years ago the Chinese made gunpowder and today they are still famous for fireworks.

Diving for the past

64 **Marine archaeology is the hunt for remains under the sea.** Untouched, the seabed can yield amazing relics of the past. Shipwrecks can be time capsules, capturing the moment the ship sunk.

65 **Marine archaeologists use robot submarines called ROVs – remotely operated vehicles.** When a shipwreck is too deep for divers to reach, an ROV is sent down to explore. Archaeologists guide the ROV from a boat on the surface. Video cameras on the submersible send back underwater pictures.

66 **Marine archaeologists "mow the lawn."** Wreck hunters can find shipwrecks hidden underwater by using sound. A sonar device can map the seafloor by bouncing sound waves off it. Archaeologists sometimes call this mapping technique "mowing the lawn."

▶ Some ROVs can bring objects back to the surface with a remote-controlled grab arm.

COMEX-PRO

67 **The Swedish warship, *Vasa*, sank on her first voyage in 1628.** The wreck was found preserved in the cold waters of Stockholm harbor in 1961. Once raised from the seabed, a museum was built around it. Scientists are trying to keep it preserved.

68 **The *Mary Rose* may have sunk because her crew could not speak English.** King Henry VIII's ship the *Mary Rose* sunk near Portsmouth in 1545. Experts think she sank when she turned sharply, letting water in through open gun holes. The ship's crew may not have understood orders to shut them!

▲ A few pieces of pirate treasure found in the wreck of the *Whydah*.

69 **Off Cape Cod in Massachusetts, divers are exploring the wreck of a real pirate ship.** The *Whydah* was the ship of pirate "Black Sam" Bellamy, and it sank in a storm in April 1717. It was said to have four tons of looted silver and gold on board. However, since the wreck was found in 1984, little silver or gold has been recovered.

▼ Lifted from the seabed, the 17th-century warship *Vasa* is on display in Stockholm, Sweden.

Time capsules

70 A time capsule is a lucky find of a collection of relics that gives a snapshot picture of a time in the past. It might be a hidden chamber undisturbed for centuries, or a box of possessions buried as someone in the past fled for their life.

71 A Stone Age garbage dump is a prehistoric time capsule. Early people moved around a lot and many of their possessions have rotted away. However, Stone Age people often left behind trash dumps called middens. This is where they threw trash, such as bones and shellfish shells after eating. Middens tell us a lot about how ancient people lived.

▲ An old well in Jamestown is a time capsule that revealed much about life for early settlers in America.

72 The first English settlers in America grew tobacco. Jamestown was set up in 1607 by 104 pioneers who sailed over from London. In 2006, archaeologists found a time capsule when they discovered a well that had been bricked up since 1617. In it they found tools, shoes and a jug belonging to the first pioneers. They also found seeds that people would have planted, including tobacco.

MAKE A TIME CAPSULE

Fill a tough plastic food storage box with small items that might tell someone about the time you live in. Label the items and write a letter to the future – remember to date it. Bury the box in your garden for archaeologists to find in the future.

FINDINGS

1. Pig's skull
2. Bartman stoneware jug
3. Earthenware pitcher
4. Iron meat cleaver
5. Iron breastplate
6. Iron burgonet helmet
7. Pewter flagon (jug)
8. Leather shoe
9. Broad ax
10. Gridiron, used over a fire

73 The cold of Siberia's Altai mountains froze the tomb of a princess. In 1993, archaeologists found the tomb of a young princess who died 2,400 years ago. The tomb was flooded soon after she was buried, then quick–frozen by the mountain ice. Like a crumbly sleeping beauty, the princess lay inside, dressed in silk and crimson wool. Lying beside her were six horses in harnesses.

▶ Usually, archaeologists only find hard things, such as pottery, but in York they found these leather shoes and a knitted sock.

74 One thousand years ago, the city of York, England, was called Jorvik by the Vikings. The damp soil beneath modern York has preserved the remains of Viking Jorvik. Archaeologists know about the shape of Viking houses, the tools they used and the games they played. They even found a Viking sock!

▼ Icy conditions and the log walls of the princess's tomb helped preserve her for 24 centuries. The princess as she may have looked (below).

Famous sites

75 Ur in Iraq was the world's first great city. Around 5,000 years ago, people called Sumerians built great cities near the Tigris and Euphrates rivers, and Ur was one of these. It was here that writing was developed. Archaeologists discovered the site in 1854.

▼ This is the city mound, or ziggurat, of ancient Ur as it looked when new 4,000 years ago. Now it is just a ruin.

76 Sites in Pakistan's Indus Valley show India had some of the world's first cities. In the 1920s, archaeologist Sir Mortimer Wheeler dug at Mohenjo-Daro, in what is now Pakistan. He found the remains of a city that was nearly 5,000 years old.

77 The Palace of Knossos, Crete, may have been home to the tyrant king, Minos. According to legend, there was a labyrinth (maze) under the palace. Young girls were sent into the maze to be killed by the terrible minotaur that lived there – a monster that was half-bull half-man. In 1899, archaeologist Arthur Evans unearthed the remains of a 4,000-year-old palace in Knossos. It may have been Minos' palace.

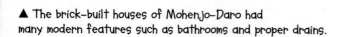

▲ The brick-built houses of Mohenjo-Daro had many modern features such as bathrooms and proper drains.

▲ The Moon Pyramid of Teotihuacán contains the remains of six smaller buildings.

78 Teotihuacán was the greatest city in the New World. Before Europeans arrived in the Americas, this civilization rose and fell in Mexico. It left a huge city, with two great pyramids dedicated to the Sun and Moon, and a vast temple for Quetzalcóatl, the feathered snake god.

79 The Parthenon in Athens, Greece, is said by some to be the world's most perfect building. It is a temple that was built by the ancient Greeks in Athens 2,400 years ago. Its graceful geometric proportions have inspired countless architects. Much of the Parthenon has fallen into ruin over the centuries and experts are now trying to restore it. Some argue this is wrong because the new parts are not authentic.

◄ The beautiful Parthenon in Athens is partially covered in scaffolding as experts carry out restoration work.

Clues from above

80 **Photographs from the air can reveal ancient sites.** From above, you can often see sites you can't see on the ground. Patterns show up where plants grow differently because the soil was disturbed in the past. Shadows of slight bumps made by the low sun at sunrise or sunset may also reveal ancient structures.

▼ The site of the lost village of Wharram Percy in Yorkshire was discovered when pictures from the air revealed slight bumps in the ground.

▶ The size and shape of the ancient circle of stones and banks at Avebury in England can only be seen clearly from the air.

81 **The lost medieval village of Wharram Percy was discovered with photos from the air.** In the Middle Ages, there were many more villages in England, but a lot were deserted as villagers fell victim to plague and hard times. On the ground, the lost villages are hard to find. But they are visible from the air as the sun picks out bumps in the ground.

TRUE OR FALSE

1. Ancient sites may be revealed by how plants grow.
2. The best time of day to take pictures from the air is midday.
3. The lines at Nazca are the remains of an ancient airport.

Answers:
1. True 2. False, the best time is just after sunrise or just before sunset 3. False

82 **The secrets of ancient farmers at Lake Titicaca were discovered from above.** The lake is almost 13,000 feet (4,000 m) above sea level, high in the Andes mountains in South America. Although it is cold and dry, it often floods, making farming difficult. Aerial photos revealed that over 3,000 years ago people farmed here using a system of raised fields. Farmers dug canals to channel water and used earth to build up fields in between. Today, local farmers are trying the system and it works!

▲ The ancient field system at Lake Titicaca was revealed by aerial photographs.

83 **Stretching across Peru, the Nazca drawings are ancient patterns that can be seen from the sky.** They depict monkeys and birds, hundreds of feet long. They were made about 1,500 years ago. No one is sure what they were for but some experts think they were walks laid out in patterns for religious reasons. No one knew they existed until planes flew over in the 1920s.

▶ The vast, ancient drawings on the ground at Nazca in Peru are only visible from the air.

Sticks and stones

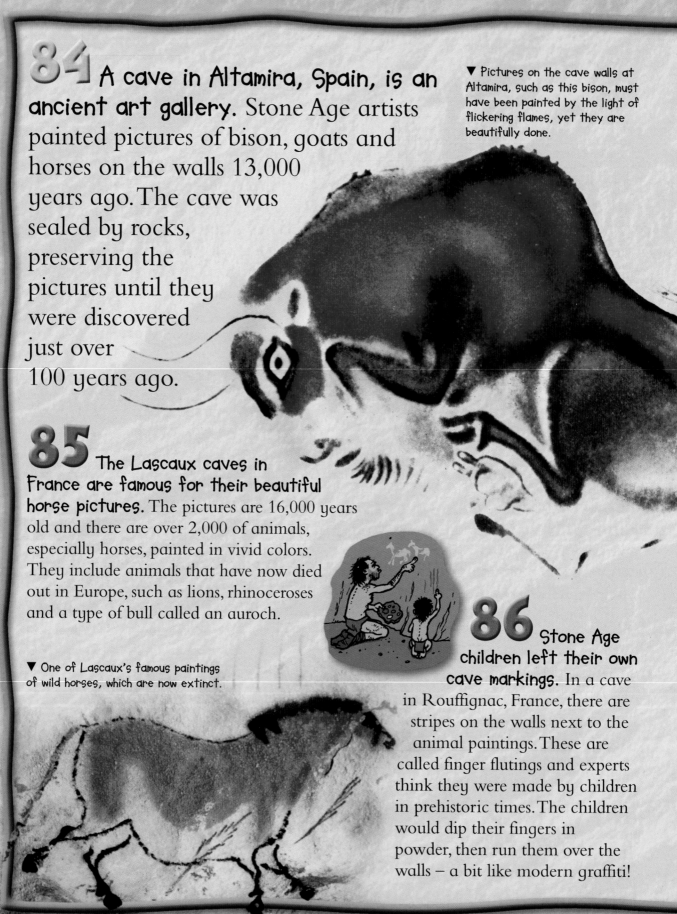

84 A cave in Altamira, Spain, is an ancient art gallery. Stone Age artists painted pictures of bison, goats and horses on the walls 13,000 years ago. The cave was sealed by rocks, preserving the pictures until they were discovered just over 100 years ago.

▼ Pictures on the cave walls at Altamira, such as this bison, must have been painted by the light of flickering flames, yet they are beautifully done.

85 The Lascaux caves in France are famous for their beautiful horse pictures. The pictures are 16,000 years old and there are over 2,000 of animals, especially horses, painted in vivid colors. They include animals that have now died out in Europe, such as lions, rhinoceroses and a type of bull called an auroch.

▼ One of Lascaux's famous paintings of wild horses, which are now extinct.

86 Stone Age children left their own cave markings. In a cave in Rouffignac, France, there are stripes on the walls next to the animal paintings. These are called finger flutings and experts think they were made by children in prehistoric times. The children would dip their fingers in powder, then run them over the walls – a bit like modern graffiti!

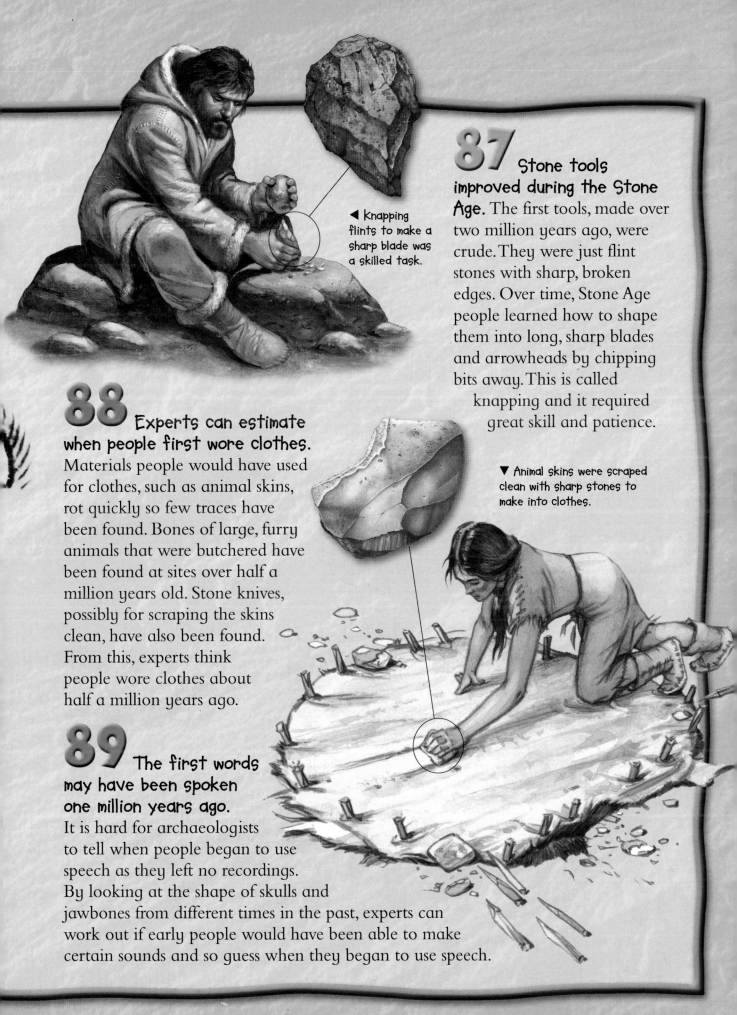

◄ Knapping flints to make a sharp blade was a skilled task.

87 Stone tools improved during the Stone Age. The first tools, made over two million years ago, were crude. They were just flint stones with sharp, broken edges. Over time, Stone Age people learned how to shape them into long, sharp blades and arrowheads by chipping bits away. This is called knapping and it required great skill and patience.

▼ Animal skins were scraped clean with sharp stones to make into clothes.

88 Experts can estimate when people first wore clothes. Materials people would have used for clothes, such as animal skins, rot quickly so few traces have been found. Bones of large, furry animals that were butchered have been found at sites over half a million years old. Stone knives, possibly for scraping the skins clean, have also been found. From this, experts think people wore clothes about half a million years ago.

89 The first words may have been spoken one million years ago. It is hard for archaeologists to tell when people began to use speech as they left no recordings. By looking at the shape of skulls and jawbones from different times in the past, experts can work out if early people would have been able to make certain sounds and so guess when they began to use speech.

Past disasters

90 An eruption preserved the Roman city of Pompeii. Mount Vesuvius erupted on August 24, AD 79, spewing out tons of ash. Archaeologists digging at Pompeii today are finding it preserved, exactly as it was on that day. Buildings, people, their pets – even their last meals are there. Two-thirds of the city's remains have been uncovered so far.

▼ Ash from the eruption of Mount Vesuvius buried nearby Pompeii so quickly, people had little time to escape.

91 On the Greek island of Santorini, an ancient city is hidden under ash. About 3,500 years ago a huge volcano exploded in the Eastern Mediterranean. It buried a Minoan city, now called Akrotiri. Archaeologists digging through the ash are finding a city full of large houses, streets and squares.

▼ A roof has been built over Akrotiri to protect the ancient remains as archaeologists uncover them.

92 **An earthquake that preserved a Native American village caused a tidal wave in Japan.** On January 5, 1700, an earthquake set off mudslides and buried the village of Ozette, Washington. Six houses were sealed under mud, preserving basketry and tools. The earthquake set off a tidal wave that swept across the Pacific to Japan, where its impact was recorded.

93 **Port Royal in Jamaica was the world's wildest city.** In the 1600s, Port Royal was where pirates went to spend their loot and have fun. On June 7, 1692, the city was hit by an earthquake and three tidal waves. Archaeologists are now digging into the seabed to find the remains of this city.

94 **In the Guatemalan jungle there is a hidden city, abandoned 1,500 years ago.** The Mayan city of Masuul (now Naachtun) was full of huge pyramids, squares and palaces. Now it is overgrown by jungle. Experts think it was abandoned during times of war.

95 **A volcanic eruption preserved the Mexican city of Cuicuilco.** When a nearby volcano erupted 1,850 years ago, the people of Cuicuilco abandoned the city. It was covered by lava and ash, 33 feet (10 m) deep. Under the lava, the city, including its giant pyramid, was preserved. It was rediscovered in the 1920s.

▶ As archaeologists discovered, not all Cuicuilco's inhabitants escaped the volcanic eruption.

Heading for America

96 The first known inhabitants of North America may have walked from Siberia. North America was joined by land to Siberia 12,000 years ago. People may have got to America by walking across this stretch of land.

Around 6,000 years ago, the bridge of land that joined Siberia to North America disappeared as sea levels rose

▲ The first Americans may have been big game hunters, following lions and elephant-like creatures into America from Siberia.

97 At Kennewick in Washington State, 9,000-year-old bones of a "European" man were found. Scientists reconstructed the face of the Kennewick Man and he looked very European. However, Christopher Columbus is said to have been the first European to reach America, yet he did not get there until 500 years ago.

98 French cavemen may have reached North America 15,000 years ago. Experts have compared 15,000-year-old stone tools found in North America with tools of the same age found in France and they look very similar. Some experts suggest that French cavemen may have crossed the Atlantic by canoe, traveling along the edge of the Arctic ice to reach America.

▼ The 9,000-year-old bones of the Kennewick Man look like those of a European, not a native American.

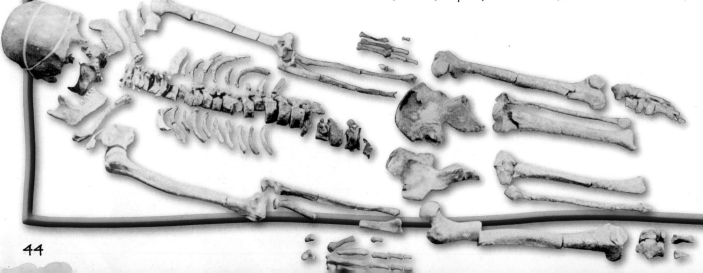

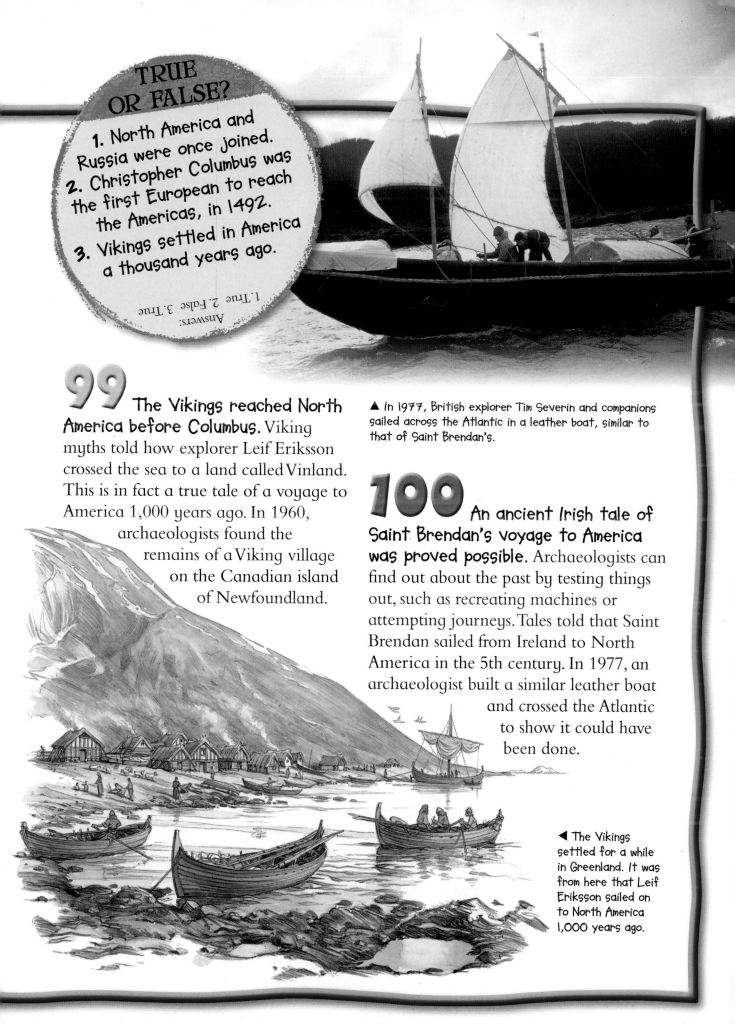

99 The Vikings reached North America before Columbus.

Viking myths told how explorer Leif Eriksson crossed the sea to a land called Vinland. This is in fact a true tale of a voyage to America 1,000 years ago. In 1960, archaeologists found the remains of a Viking village on the Canadian island of Newfoundland.

▲ In 1977, British explorer Tim Severin and companions sailed across the Atlantic in a leather boat, similar to that of Saint Brendan's.

100 An ancient Irish tale of Saint Brendan's voyage to America was proved possible.

Archaeologists can find out about the past by testing things out, such as recreating machines or attempting journeys. Tales told that Saint Brendan sailed from Ireland to North America in the 5th century. In 1977, an archaeologist built a similar leather boat and crossed the Atlantic to show it could have been done.

◀ The Vikings settled for a while in Greenland. It was from here that Leif Eriksson sailed on to North America 1,000 years ago.

Glossary

afterlife: an existence after death

amphora: an ancient Greek jar or vase with a large oval body, narrow cylindrical neck, and two handles that rise almost to the level of the mouth

ancestor: a precursor of a more recent or existing species or group

archaeologist: a scientist who studies past human life and activities

debris: the remains of something that has been broken

hieroglyphics: the picture script of ancient Egypt

midden: a historical waste pile

oracle: advice from god

peat bog: wet spongy ground containing matter left over from plants that have partly broken down in water

smelt: to melt or fuse (as ore) often with an accompanying chemical change usually to separate the metal

submersible: a usually small underwater craft used especially for deep-sea research

terracotta: a glazed or unglazed fired clay used especially for statuettes and vases and architectural purposes

thermoluminescence: phosphorescence (glowing) developed in a previously excited substance upon gentle heating, and the determination of the age of old material (as pottery) by the amount of thermoluminescence it produces

time capsule: a container holding historical records or objects representative of current culture that is deposited (as in a cornerstone) for preservation until discovery by some future age

trowel: a scoop-shaped or flat-bladed garden tool for taking up and setting small plants or buried objects

For More Information

Books

Athans, Sandra. *Secrets of the Sky Caves*. Minneapolis, MN: Millbrook Press, 2014.

Carman, John, Carol McDavid, and Robin Skeates. *The Oxford Handbook of Public Archaeology*. New York: Oxford, 2012.

Hunter, Nick. *Ancient Treasures*. North Mankato, MN: Capstone, 2014.

Websites

Jamestown Rediscovery
http://historicjamestowne.org/archaeology/dig-updates/
Tour a historical dig of Jamestown, Virginia, one of the first cities in the American colonies.

Mummy Bundles of Puruchuco
http://channel.nationalgeographic.com/channel/content/inca/
Follow along a journey to find mummies in Peru.

NPS Archaeology for Kids
http://www.nps.gov/Archeology/public/kids/index.htm
Check out this National Park Service archaeology program website.

Index

Page numbers in **bold** refer to main subject entries. Page numbers in *italics* refer to illustrations.